FRANCE

by Bitsy Kemper

The Child's World

Published by The Child's World®
1980 Lookout Drive • Mankato, MN 56003-1705
800-599-READ • www.childsworld.com

Acknowledgments
The Child's World®: Mary Berendes, Publishing Director
Red Line Editorial: Editorial direction
The Design Lab: Design
Amnet: Production

Design elements: Claudio Divizia/Shutterstock Images; Shutterstock Images
Photographs ©: Ekaterina Pokrovsky/Shutterstock Images, cover (right); Claudio
Divizia/Shutterstock Images, cover (left center), 1 (bottom left), 18 (left); Shutterstock
Images, cover (left top), cover (left bottom), 1 (top), 1 (bottom right), 18 (right), 25;
iStockphoto, 5, 6–7, 10, 11, 12, 13, 20, 26, 30; Xavier Arnau/iStockphoto, 8;
Anya Ivanova/iStockphoto, 15; Viacheslav Lopatin/Shutterstock Images, 16; Andrew
Howe/iStockphoto, 17; Botond Horvath/Shutterstock Images, 21; Evgeny Prokofyev/
Shutterstock Images, 22; Nanette Grebe/iStockphoto, 23; Alesya Novikova/
Shutterstock Images, 24; Franck Boston/Shutterstock Images, 27; Photos.com/
Thinkstock, 28

ISBN 9781634070430
LCCN 2014959727

Printed in the United States of America
PA02345

ABOUT THE AUTHOR

Bitsy Kemper has written more than a dozen books. She's active in sports, church, and theater (but not all at the same time). Kemper loves a good laugh as much as a good read. Busy with three kids, she also enjoys learning about new cultures.

ONE WORLD • MANY COUNTRIES

TABLE OF CONTENTS

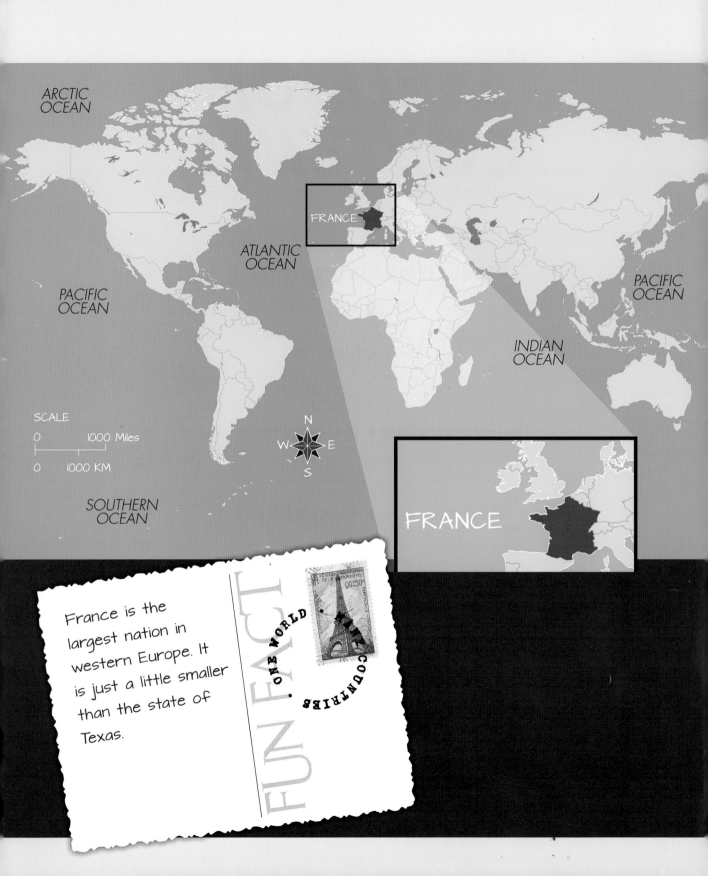

ARCTIC
OCEAN

FRANCE

ATLANTIC
OCEAN

PACIFIC
OCEAN

PACIFIC
OCEAN

INDIAN
OCEAN

SCALE

0   1000 Miles

0   1000 KM

N
W   E
S

SOUTHERN
OCEAN

FRANCE

FUN FACT

France is the largest nation in western Europe. It is just a little smaller than the state of Texas.

ONE WORLD · MANY COUNTRIES

CHAPTER 1

WELCOME TO FRANCE!

Crowds are growing bigger. They line the street ten people deep. Dozens of people trot by on horses. The riders are playing horns and drums. Flags of 28 European countries blow in the wind.

The president drives by and waves. Army tanks roll down the street. Soon an airshow begins as fighter jets fly across the sky. Soldiers march, fire trucks cruise by, and helicopters fly in formation to end the parade.

Fighter jets spray trails of red, white, and blue during the Bastille Day parade. They are the colors of the French flag.

Later that night people gather to watch fireworks bursting over the Eiffel Tower. The parades and fireworks are all part of Bastille Day. France celebrates the holiday on July 14. It honors *La Fête Nationale*, when the French people rebelled against the king and queen in 1789. It was the start of the French Revolution. The revolution gave citizens more power. It ended the royal rule.

Bastille Day honors this important day in French

history. The French have great pride in their traditions and culture. Their artists, writers, and musicians have influenced world. Their buildings are known for their grace and beauty. French food is considered by many people to be some of the world's finest. In many ways, this small European country has had a large impact on the world.

The Eiffel Tower is one of France's most famous structures.

CHAPTER 2

THE LAND

Thousands of years ago, glaciers in the Pyrenees melted and formed lakes.

France is in Europe. To its south, France borders Spain, Andorra, and the Mediterranean Sea. In the north, the English Channel separates France and Great Britain. Western France has a long coast along the Bay of Biscay. To the east, France neighbors Italy, Switzerland, and Germany. Northeastern France borders Luxembourg and Belgium.

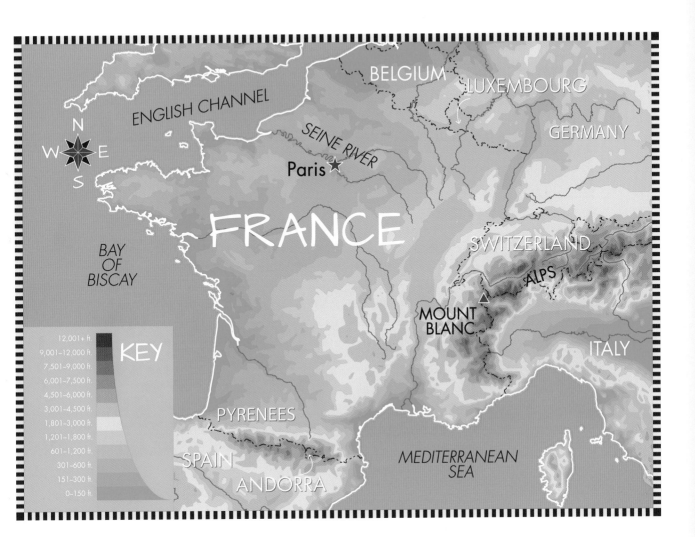

Mountains rise across western France. They are the Pyrenees. The Pyrenees stretch for 270 miles (430 km). They form the border between France and Spain. Mountain passes allow people to cross from one side to the other.

The Alps are another mountain range. They are in eastern France. These mountains form the border between France and

The Seine River flows through Paris.

Italy. The tallest peak is Mont Blanc. It is 15,771 feet (4,807 m) tall. The mountain is so big, that it is part of France, Italy, and Switzerland.

The Seine River flows across central France. It begins as a stream near the city of Dijon. It flows northwest, eventually reaching Paris. It flows through Paris and into the English Channel.

The Seine River is important to France. It links Paris with the sea. Many boats travel along it every day. The Seine also provides drinking water for much of Paris. The first settlement in Paris was on an island in the Seine.

Plains and gently rolling hills cover much of the country. This land has rich soil for farming. Farmers grow crops such as wheat, corn, and grapes. These foods are used in France and sold to other countries.

France is famous for its grapes, which are made into wine.

France's land is also rich with trees. The country has one of the largest forested areas in Europe. Some of its wood is made into paper, boards, and timber. France's forestry industry provides jobs to about 80,000 people each year.

Winters in France are cool. Summers are mild. From October to April the weather is misty. Along the Mediterranean coast, the weather is warmer. This area has strong, cold winds in the winter and spring.

Le Tour de France is an international bicycle race through France every year. Over several weeks, bikers ride more than 2,000 miles (3,220 km).

FUN FACT · ONE WORLD · MANY COUNTRIES

CHAPTER 3

GOVERNMENT AND CITIES

The French government meets in Paris. It is the nation's capital.

The French **Republic** is France's official name. It is divided into 27 regions. The regions are similar to states. Five of France's regions are not in Europe. These areas are in other parts of the world. French Guiana is in South America. Guadeloupe

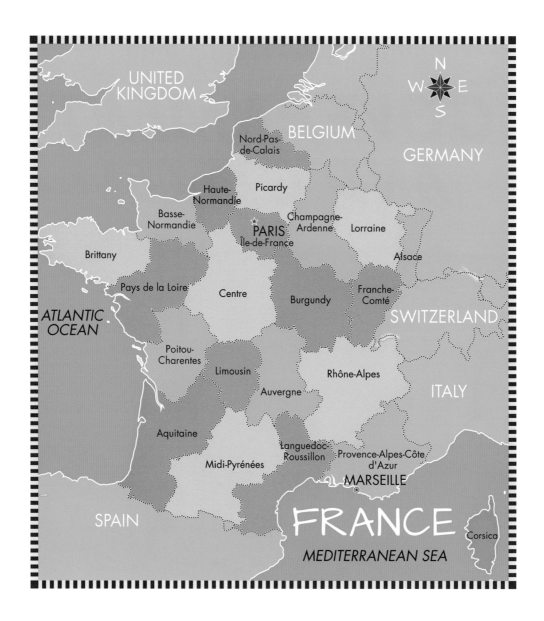

and Martinique are islands in the Caribbean Sea. Mayotte and Réunion are islands off the coast of Africa.

French citizens vote for their president. The president leads the military, works with lawmakers, and appoints **ambassadors**. The president also chooses France's prime minister. The prime minister leads the government, which includes lawmakers. Lawmakers serve in the **parliament**.

The government meets in Paris. Paris is the capital and largest city in France. About 11 million people live there. It is a city that is full of history, culture, and art. Its nickname is the

The Arc de Triomphe was completed in 1836.

City of Light. This is because it is a center of learning and ideas. It was also the first European city to have streetlights.

One of the most famous streets in Paris is the Champs-Élysées. It is 1.2 miles (1.9 km) long. It begins at the Arc de Triomphe. This large arch is a **monument**. It honors the victories of the French military. At the other end of the Champs-Élysées is a large, open square. It is called the Place de la Concorde. Shops and gardens also line this famous street.

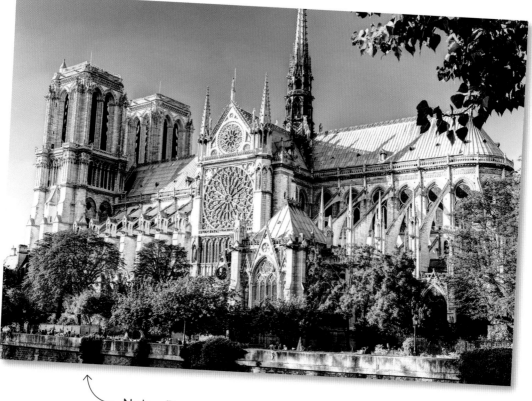

Notre-Dame Cathedral

Paris has many famous buildings, too. The Eiffel Tower was built for the 1889 World's Fair. It is 986 feet (301 m) tall. Today the building is a symbol of Paris known around the world. The Notre-Dame Cathedral in Paris has been in use since 1272. People come from all over to see its beautiful stained glass windows and historic **architecture**.

Paris has the world's most-visited museum. It is the Musée du Louvre. Each year, more than 9 million people walk through its galleries. The Mona Lisa by Leonardo da Vinci is one of its famous works of art.

FUN FACT

ONE WORLD · MANY COUNTRIES

To the south of Paris is the city of Marseilles. This city is located along the Mediterranean Sea. It has the country's largest port. Most of the ships arriving in the port carry **imports** from other countries. The most common imports are oil, natural gas, and building materials.

France **exports** goods, too. It is famous for its wine. Much of this wine is exported to other countries. France also exports machines, aircraft, plastics, and chemicals. Its most important trading partners are Germany, Belgium, and Italy.

France's currency

France's flag

GLOBAL CONNECTIONS

France is a popular country for tourists. More than 84 million people visit every year. This makes it the world's most-visited country. It also means France has more tourists than locals. About 80 percent of the people who travel to France are from other European countries.

People travel to France for many reasons. Some travel to southern France to enjoy the warm weather. This area is home to the Côte d'Azur, or French Riviera. The Côte d'Azur has beautiful beaches. People swim and sunbathe. They also go boating, diving, and fishing.

People also travel to France for the food and wine. They try some fresh-baked French breads, such as *baguettes* and *croissants*. Or, they may sample some of the country's 400 kinds of cheeses. Other tourists go to vineyards, where they can sample France's famous wines.

France's mountains also draw visitors. In the summer, people enjoy hiking and climbing in the Alps and the Pyrenees. In the winter, these same mountains are popular for downhill skiing and snowboarding.

Fine arts also attract tourists. People enjoy visiting France's many museums. They may spend an evening listening to music at the Paris Opera House. Touring the nation's beautiful cathedrals and admiring the architecture, stained glass, and paintings is also popular.

CHAPTER 4

PEOPLE AND CULTURES

In France, outdoor cafés are popular places to have coffee or eat a meal.

People have lived in France for thousands of years. Around 250 BC, a tribe called the Celt Parisii moved to France. The city of Paris is named after this tribe. Romans and Germans also ruled France. Today, French people are a mix of all these groups.

Nearly everyone in France speaks French. It is the country's official language. French is used in schools, businesses, and government. Some French people also speak regional languages. In Brittany, people speak Breton. In southern France people speak Provençal.

French people practice many different religions. The majority of French people are Roman Catholic. About 5 million people practice Islam. Many of them are **immigrants** from North Africa. Many people in France also practice Judaism.

Catholics attend Mass at a cathedral in Strasbourg, France.

Soldiers in Montpellier, France, march in a parade to honor veterans on Victory Day.

In France, people practice many local customs. Upon meeting a friend, a French person will often kiss his friend once on each cheek. This is called *faire la bise*, which means "to give a kiss." At mealtime, people do not eat until the host says, *bon appétit*. It means "good appetite," and it is a wish for an enjoyable meal.

The French celebrate many holidays. One of the most important religious holidays is Christmas. Families often display a *crèche de Noël* in their homes. It is a nativity scene that shows the people of the Christmas story. Many people attend a midnight **Mass** on Christmas Eve.

The French also celebrate public holidays. World War II Victory Day is celebrated on May 8. Flags are proudly displayed around the country. Soldiers of today and the past are remembered and honored.

FUN FACT · ONE WORLD · MANY COUNTRIES

In 1581, dancers performed the world's first ballet for French royalty. Ballet grew in popularity, and France's King Louis XIV opened a ballet school in 1661. It was called the Académie Royale de Danse. Dancers who studied there created the movements used in classical ballet today.

CHAPTER 5

DAILY LIFE

In France, people enjoy spending time outside and relaxing.

Daily life in France is often centered on finding balance. The balance is between work and other enjoyable activities, such as cooking or spending time with friends. On average, the French work 35 hours per week. In 2014, a law ruled that companies could not make employees answer e-mails or calls after 6 p.m.

When not working, the French might wander through outdoor markets. Smaller towns may hold markets once a week. Larger towns and cities hold daily markets. Markets offer local foods such as fresh olives, garden plants, and honey. Some sell special foods from other countries.

Fine foods are an important part of daily life. France brought the world *croissants*, *crêpes*, and olive relish. Coffee

Meals in France usually include a main dish, as well as a cheese course, a vegetable course, and a desert.

breaks are an important part of everyday life, too. Small cafés line many French streets.

People can get around France in many ways. They can walk or take a train, bus, or taxi. In Paris, people can ride the Métro. It is the city's subway system. Riding bicycles is also common.

Bicycling is a common way to get from place to place in Paris.

Traditional apartments in Paris are made of brick. The upper stories usually have large windows and balconies.

Many bicycles have baskets on the handlebars. They are good for holding groceries or other items.

Homes in France vary greatly. In large cities, people often live in apartment buildings. Some apartment buildings in Paris have been around for hundreds of years. The city also has many modern apartment buildings. In rural areas, families often live in single-family homes.

Fashion is important in France. Many French people take great care in how they dress. Clothing is often simple, elegant, and well-fitted. It is often more formal than what is worn in the United States. Women wear skirts, dresses, and pants. Men wear shirts, sweaters, and pants.

FUN FACT

Claude Monet is a famous painter from France. His art focuses on the way light and color mix together.

ONE WORLD COUNTRIES

From fashion to food, France has had a lasting impact. Its culture, art, and language have shaped what many people consider refined and beautiful. Its people take great pride in all France has given to the world.

DAILY LIFE FOR CHILDREN

French children begin attending school at age six. They attend *école primaire*, or elementary school. Their school days are much like children in other parts of the world. They study math, reading, science, and music.

At lunch, students eat in the *restaurant scolaire*, or student restaurant. Students sit at tables and are served four courses. The first course is often a vegetable, such as carrot salad. Next the children have a main course, such as fish or chicken. Then they have a cheese course and dessert. Children are encouraged to eat slowly and enjoy the meal.

When not in school, French children enjoy spending time with their friends. They may play a game of soccer or ride their bicycles. Some children enjoy playing *la marelle ronde*, a traditional game similar to hopscotch.

FAST FACTS

Population: 66 million

Area: 248,573 square miles (643,801 sq km)

Capital: Paris

Largest Cities: Paris, Marseille-Aix-en-Provence, and Lyon

Form of Government: Republic

Language: French

Trading Partners:
Germany, Belgium, and Italy

Major Holidays:t
Christmas, Bastille Day, and
World War II Victory Day

National Dish: *Pot-au-Feu* (a stew of beef, root vegetables, and spices)

Provence, France, is famous for its lavender fields. The plants have bright purple blooms in the summer.

GLOSSARY

ambassadors (am-BASS-uh-duhrs) Officials who represent their country while living elsewhere. France's president appoints ambassadors.

architecture (AR-kih-tek-chur) The style or elements of a building. France has many famous pieces of architecture.

exports (ek-SPORTS) When a country exports goods, it sells them to other countries. France exports many products to the other countries in Europe.

immigrants (IM-ih-grunts) Immigrants are people who move to a foreign country to live. France has many immigrants.

imports (ihm-PORTs) Imports are goods brought into another country to trade or sell. France imports many goods.

Mass (mass) A Mass is a service in the Catholic Church. Many French people attend a midnight Mass on Christmas Eve.

monument (MAHN-yuh-ment) A monument is a building, statue, or other item made to remember a person or event. The Arc de Triomphe is a monument to France's soldiers.

parliament (PAR-luh-ment) Parliament is a group of elected officials that makes laws. France has a parliament.

republic (ree-PUB-lick) A republic is a country with a government in which people elect officials to manage the government. France is a republic.

TO LEARN MORE

BOOKS

Lamprell, Klay. *Not-for-Parents Paris: Everything You Ever Wanted to Know*. Oakland, CA: Lonely Planet, 2011.

Pezzi, Bryan. *Eiffel Tower*. New York: Weigl Publishers, 2008.

Ray, Michael. *France*. New York: Britannica Educational Publishing, 2014.

WEB SITES

Visit our Web site for links about France: **childsworld.com/links**

Note to Parents, Teachers, and Librarians: We routinely verify our Web links to make sure they are safe and active sites. So encourage your readers to check them out!

INDEX